CATALOG OF ROYCROFT FURNITURE AND OTHER THINGS

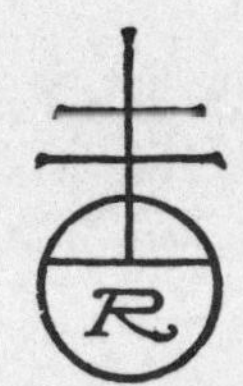

PRINTED BY THE ROYCROFTERS, AT THEIR PRINT SHOP, WHICH IS IN EAST AURORA, ERIE COUNTY, NEW YORK STATE, U. S. A., A. D., MCMVI

Reprinted from original catalogue.

Roycroft Furniture and Other Things

OYCROFT FURNITURE is individual. It is appreciated for its attractiveness, its purity of design, its symmetrical lines, mechanical construction, and the rich, soft colors in the woods and finishes. These make a combination which brings lasting joy, for each piece is a classic ❧ Our lumber is all specially prepared, being air-dried from two to five years, according to thickness, then kiln-dried for three months at a temperature of One Hundred and Sixty degrees, thus retaining to a great extent the lifelike appearance and natural strength of the woods.

We would ask you not to class our products as "Mission," or so-called "Mission Furniture." Ours is purely **Roycroft**—made by us according to our own ideas. We have eliminated all unnecessary elaboration, but have kept in view the principles of artistic quality, sound mechanical construction and good workmanship.

WOOD.—We make our **Furniture** in Quartered Oak, Mahogany from Santo Domingo and Africa, and native White Ash, and we have the following in stock: Oak—dark, medium and light weathered; Roycroft brown, Flemish, Golden, and Japanese gray. Mahogany—dark, medium and light. Ash—brown, Japanese gray and silver gray, all done in dull wax finish, each one emphasizing the natural beauty of the wood.

LEATHER.—All padded leather seats are made of heavy cowhide, colored to match the wood, and by our special treatment are made soft and pliable—practically indestructible—and are fastened on with large-headed copper tacks or nails.

All upholstered pieces have spring seats. The leather is American russet and India cowhide, and is very soft and pliable, and at the same time is the best wearing material known for this purpose.

TRIMMINGS.—The trimmings of our **Furniture** are all made of hand-wrought copper or iron, by our own workmen, and are very near perfection, both from an artistic and mechanical standpoint.

GLASS.—All small lights of glass are clear French papered stock; all large lights are plain polished plate. All coppered glass is made in design, with clear sheet glass and heavy ribbed copper, being almost as rigid as plate glass.

For lamp shades we use the best imported opalescent glass, which has a wonderfully pleasing color. These are made in both plain and leaded, the latter being made by our own artists from special designs.

No. 055. Chafing Dish Cabinet
Coppered glass and copper trimmings
24 inches wide 16 inches deep 40 inches high
Oak, $28.00 Mahogany, $33.00 Ash, $26.00

No. 070. Table Lamp. Gas
Hand-wrought iron, wood base
$8.00

No. 049. Tabouret
14 x 14 inches top 20 in. high
Oak, $9.00 Mahogany, $11.00
Ash, $8.50

No. 05. China Cabinet
Sheet glass set in copper in doors and ends.
48 inches wide 20 inches deep 60 inches high
Oak, $70.00 Mahogany, $85.00 Ash, $66.00

No. 0108. Dresser. Swinging mirror, 34 x 28 inches
45 inches wide 24 inches deep 32 inches high
Oak, $48.00 Mahogany, $60.00 Ash, $45.00

No. 096. Carved Mahogany Chest
Cedar lined. Hand-wrought copper trimmings
42 inches wide 24 inches deep 25 inches high
Made only on order. Price, $175.00

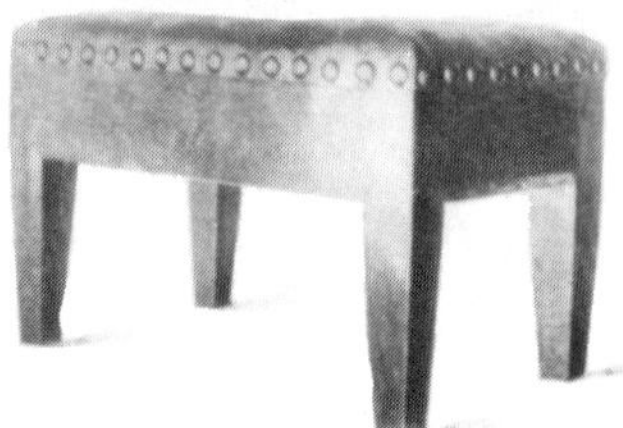

No. 048. Footstool. Leather covered
15 in. wide 9 in. deep 9½ in. high
Oak, $5.00 Mahogany, $6.00 Ash, $4.75

No. 0116. Bookrack
6 inches wide 15 inches long
Oak, $1.50 Mahogany, $1.75 Ash, $1.50

No. 0117. Bookracks
Oak, $4.50 Mahogany, $5.50

No. 02. Sideboard
66 inches wide 26 inches deep 38 inches high to shelf
Oak, $70.00 Mahogany, $85.00 Ash, $66.00
Mirror panel, $6.00 extra

No. 079. Magazine Rack
16 x 18 in. base 13 x 15 in. top
50 inches high
Oak, $16.00 Mahogany, $20.00
Ash, $14.00

No. 0111. Commode
40 inches wide 20 inches deep 28 inches high
Oak, $34.00 Mahogany, $42.00 Ash, $32.00

No. 098. Bride's Chest. Copper trimmed
36 inches wide 21 inches deep 19 inches high
Oak, $28.00 Mahogany, $35.00 Ash, $26.00

No. 097. Bride's Chest
40 inches wide 21 inches deep 26 inches high
Oak, $30.00 Mahogany, $37.00 Ash, $28.00

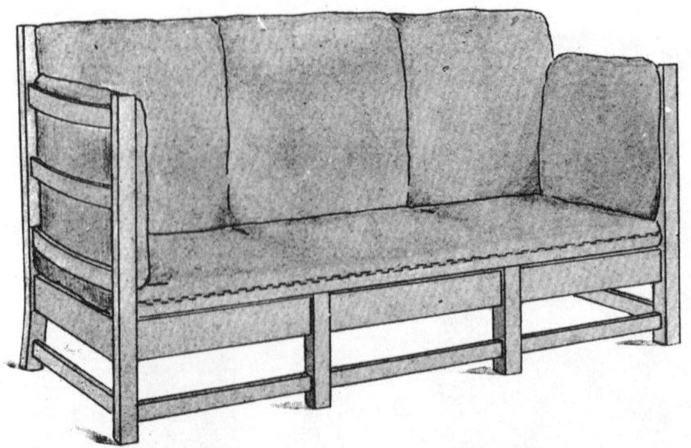

No. 054. Davenport. Leather cushions, spring seat
78 in. long 30 in. deep 16 in. to seat 26-in. back 20-in. ends
Oak, $120.00 Mahogany, $135.00 Ash, $110.00

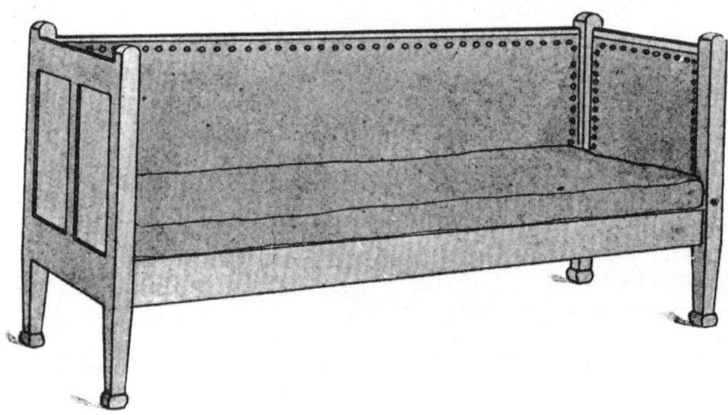

No. 052. Davenport. Leather cushion and back, spring seat
78 in. long 24 in. deep 16½ in. high to seat 20-in. back
Oak, $75.00 Mahogany, $90.00 Ash, $70.00

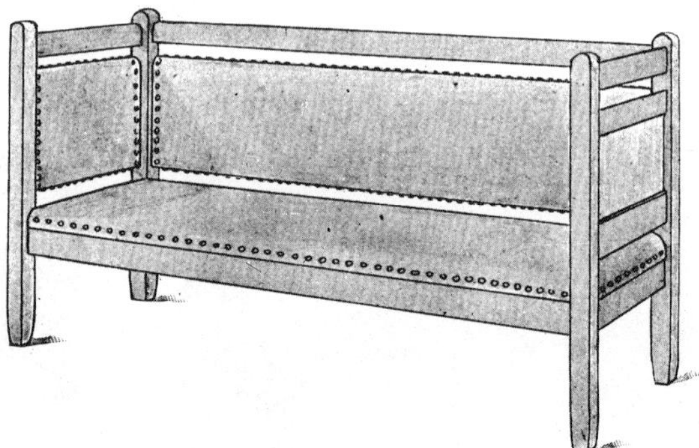

No. 053. Davenport. Leather cushions and back, spring seat
66 in. long 24 in. deep 16½ in. high to seat 24-in. back
Oak, $60.00 Mahogany, $75.00 Ash, $55.00

No. 066½. Chandelier
Copper frame and chains, opalescent glass shades
Electric, $45.00 Gas, $48.00

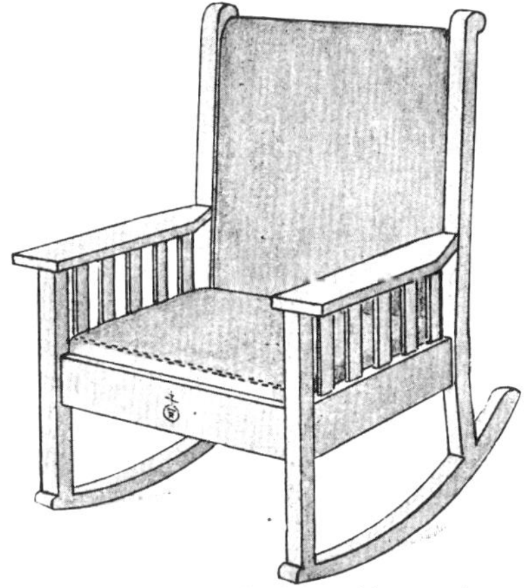

No. 051. Arm Rocker, leather cushions, spring seat
26 inches wide 22 inches deep 24-inch back
Oak, $40.00 Mahogany, $46.00 Ash, $38.00

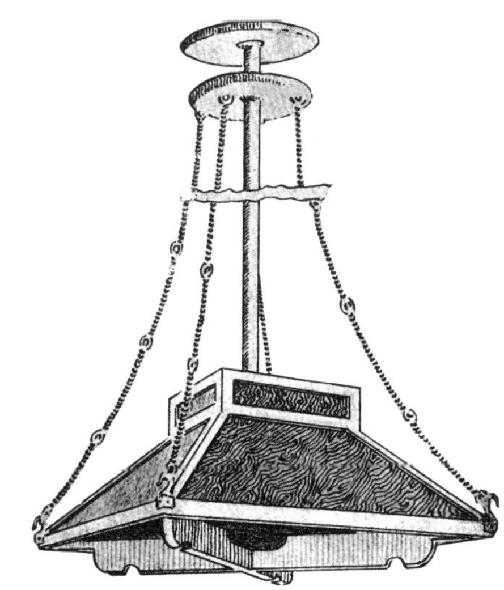

No. 066A. Chandelier
Oak frame, copper chains and fittings,
opalescent glass shades
Electric, $52.00 Gas, $58.00

No. 063. Music Cabinet

28 inches wide 16 inches deep 42 inches high

Oak, $22.00 Mahogany, $27.00 Ash, $20.00

No. 09. Combination Serving Table and Buffet

56 inches wide 22 inches deep 38 inches high to shelf

Oak, $48.00 Mahogany, $60.00 Ash, $45.00

No. 050. Tabouret
16 x 16 inch top 21 inches high
Oak, $8.00 Mahogany, $10.00 Ash $7.50

No. 050½. Tabouret. 12 x 12 inch top, 20 inches high
Oak, $5.00 Mahogany, $6.25 Ash, $5.00
Iron flower-pot holder, $3.00

No. 03. Sideboard. 16-inch mirror
62 inches wide 26 inches deep 36 inches high to center shelf
Oak, $65.00 Mahogany, $80.00 Ash, $61.00

No. 047. Footstool
20 in. wide 15 in. deep
21 in. high
Leather top One drawer
Oak, $12.00 Ash, $11.00
Mahogany, $14.50

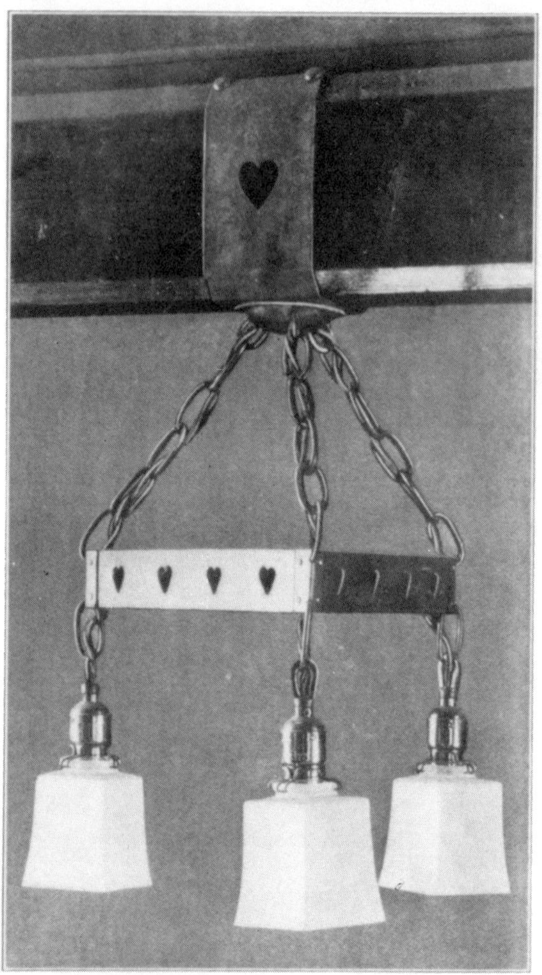

No. 065. Electric Chandelier. Three lights
Frame and chains hand-wrought copper, fitted for hanging on ceiling, $25.00

No. 080. Magazine Pedestal
18 x 18 inch base, 14½ x 14½ inch top, 63 inches high
Oak, $22.00 Mahogany, $27.50
Ash, $20.00

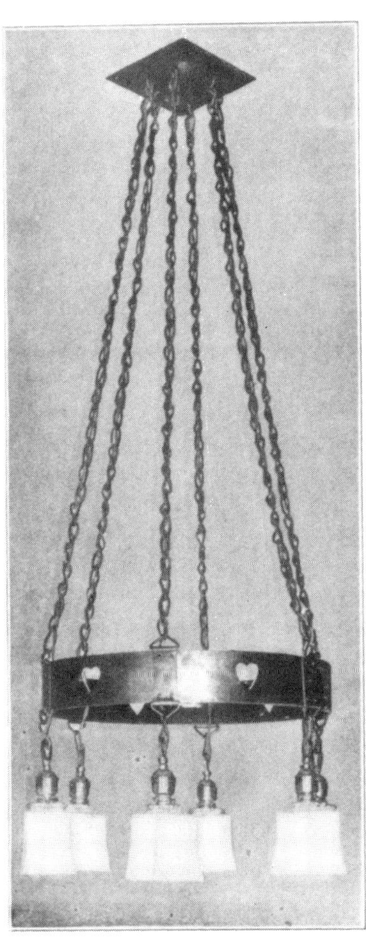

No. 066. Electric Chandelier. Six lights
Frame and chains hand-wrought copper
$38.00

No. 07½ China Cabinet
48 inches wide 56 inches high 20 inches deep
Copper set glass (in doors and ends), Plate glass shelves, mirror back
Oak, $130.00 Mahogany, $150.00 Ash, $122.00

No. 069½. Andirons. Hand-wrought iron, $20.00

No. 084. Bookcase

32 inches wide — 60 inches high — 13½ inches deep

Oak, $35.00 — Mahogany, $42.00 — Ash, $33.00

No. 019. Cellarette

40 inches wide — 18 inches deep — 34 inches high

Oak, $42.00 — Mahogany, $50.00 — Ash, $40.00

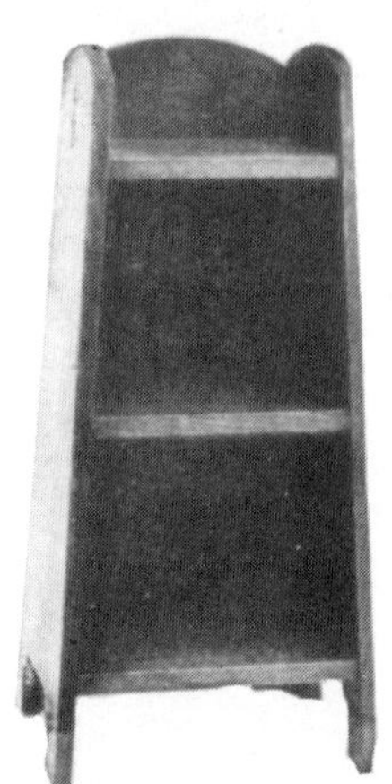

No. 078. Magazine Rack

18 x 18 inch Base, 14 x 14 inch top, 37 in. high

Oak, $10.00 — Ash, $9.00

Mahogany, $12.50

No. 08. China Cabinet and Serving Table combined
42 inches wide 20 inches deep 38 inches high to shelf
Oak, $40.00 Mahogany, $48.00 Ash, $38.00

No. 0113. Chiffonier
41½ inches wide 24 inches deep 52 inches high
Oak, $42.00 Mahogany, $52.00 Ash, $40.00

No. 018. Cellarette
Fitted with ice cooler and revolving bottle tray
40 inches wide, 20 inches deep, 41 inches high
Oak, $40.00 Mahogany, $48.00 Ash, $38.00

No. 06. China Cabinet
56 inches wide 20 inches deep 58 inches high
Oak, $72.00 Mahogany, $86.00 Ash, $68.00

No. 068. Andirons. Hand-wrought iron, $50.00
Made in sizes to suit your fireplace

No. 069. Andirons. Hand-wrought iron, $50.00
Made in sizes to suit your fireplace

MACHINE FLOOR IN FURNITURE SHOP

BENCH FLOOR IN FURNITURE SHOP

No. 0126. Roycroft Table Lamp

Fitted complete, $75.00

Landscape, Heraldic, and Aquatic Designs

The wood frame is of Oak, finished in dull, dark brown. Hand-wrought copper brackets support the shade. The panels and shades are leaded, opalescent glass

No. 011. Serving Table
Semi-Circle
48 in. wide, 24 in. deep, 36 in. high
Oak, $12.00 Mahogany, $15.00 Ash, $10.00

No. 075. Library Table
52 in. wide, 33 in. deep, 30 in. high
Oak, $38.00 Mahogany, $45.00
Ash, $35.00

No. 014. Extension Dining Table
48 in. Diameter, Open, 8 feet
Oak, $58.00 Mahogany, $68.00 Ash, $55.00

No. 041. Rocking Chair
21 x 19½ in. Leather Seat
38 in. high
Oak, $16.00 Mahogany, $20.00 Ash, $15.00

No. 041½. Rocking Chair
Same Style as No. 041
19 x 17½ in. Seat 38 in. high
Oak, $16.00 Mahogany, $20.00 Ash, $15.00

No. 093. Settee
52 in. wide, 21 in. deep
40 in. high, Wood Seat
Oak, $32.00
Mahogany, $40.00
Ash, $30.00

No. 033. Hall Chair
20 in. wide, 20 in. deep, 46 in. high
Wood Seat
Oak, $20.00 Mahogany, $25.00 Ash, $18.00

No. 028. Arm Chair
25 in. wide, 22 in. deep, 38 in. high
Leather Seat
Oak, $15.00 Mahogany, $18.00 Ash, $14.00

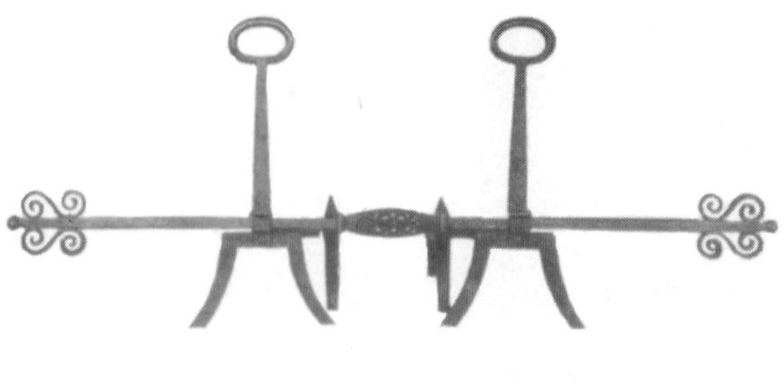

No. 0118. Hand-wrought Copper Paper Knife, 50 cents

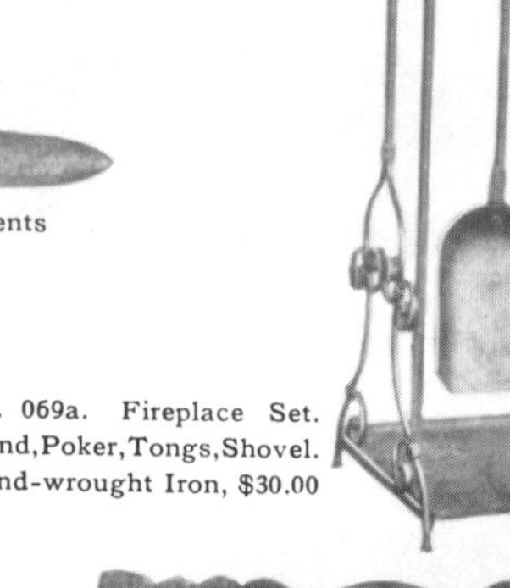

No. 069a. Fireplace Set.
Stand, Poker, Tongs, Shovel.
Hand-wrought Iron, $30.00

No. 0127. Porch Lamp

	Iron	Copper
Plain Glass, Electric	$23.00	$30.00
Opalescent Glass, Electric	25.00	32.00
Plain Glass, Gas	25.00	32.00
Opalescent Glass, Gas	27.00	34.00

No. 0120. Hand-wrought Copper Pin Tray
Size, 4 x 6½ inches; $2.00

No. 09½. Combination Buffet and Serving Table
Coppered glass doors
40 inches wide 22 inches deep 38 inches high
Oak, $36.00 Mahogany, $43.00 Ash, $34.00

No. 051a. Rocking Chair
Leather cushions, spring seat. 22 x 19-inch seat. 28-inch back
Oak, $38.00 Ash, $36.00
Mahogany, $44.00

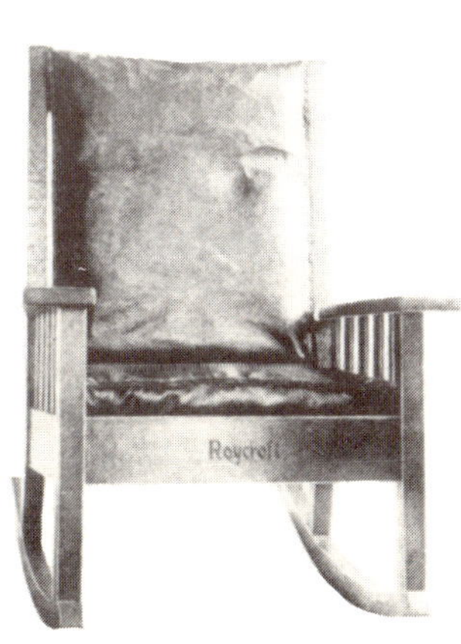

No. 051b. Rocking Chair
Same style as 051a being one size larger
Oak, $40.00 Ash, $38.00
Mahogany, $47.00

Hand-tooled and Embossed leather covered Chair $125.00

No. 059½. Table Desk
60 in. wide, 30 in. deep
30 in. high
Oak, $52.00
Mahogany, $62.00
Ash, $50.00

No. 032. Corner Chair
22 in. square, 38 in. high
Spring Seat and Padded Back—Leather
Oak, $30.00 Mahogany, $36.00
Ash, $28.00

No. 090. Ladies' desk and Chair, in A.C. design
Price for two pieces—Oak, $42.00 Mahogany, $52.00
Ash, $38.00

No. 073. Round Table
36 inches in diameter 30 inches high
Oak, $25.00 Mahogany, $30.00 Ash, $23.00

No. 044. Morris Chair Seat 21x21 inches

Oak,	Velour Cushions, $40.00	Leather, $50.00
Mahogany,	" " $48.00	" $58.00
Ash,	" " $36.00	" $46.00

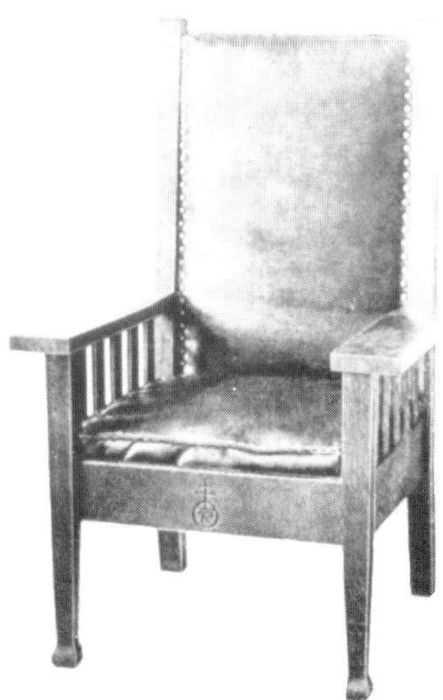

No. 034. Arm Chair
Leather cushion, spring seat, padded back
46 in. high Seat 24x24 inches
Oak, $40.00; Mahogany, $48.00; Ash, $38.00

No. 074. Round Table

30 in. diameter, 29 in. high	36 in. diameter, 30 in. high
Oak, $25.00; Ash, $23.00	Oak, $27.00; Ash, $25.00
Mahogany, $30.00	Mahogany, $33.00

No. 045. Morris Chair
25x23-in. Seat
Oak, Velour Cushions, $45.00
Leather Cushions, $55.00
Mahogany, Velour Cushions, $52.00
Leather Cushions, $62.00
Ash, Velour Cushions, $43.00
Leather Cushions, $53.00

No. 043. Moiris Chair
24 x 22-inch Seat, Rachet Adjustment
Oak, Velour Cushions, $45.00; Leather, $55.00
Mahogany, Velour Cushions, $52.00
Leather, $62.00
Ash, Velour Cushions, $43.00; Leather, 53.00

No 086. Thirty-third Degree Bookcase

40 inches wide 55 inches high 14 inches deep

Oak, $30.00 Mahogany, $37.00 Ash, $28.00

No. 086½. Same Bookcase as No. 086, excepting door, which is copper set glass

Oak, $38.00 Mahogany, $45.00 Ash, $36.00

No. 036. Child's High Chair

With name carved on back

Oak, $12.50 Mahogany, $15.00

Ash, $11.50

No. 046. Ali Baba Bench

Seat made of white ash slab. Polished top, bark side down

Legs, Oak or Ash, $10.00

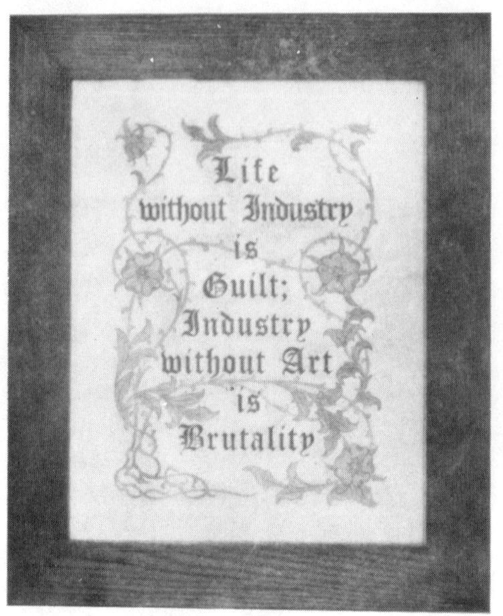

No. 0121. Oak Framed, Hand Illumined Motto
15 x 18 in. Price $2.50

No. 0125. Desk Pad—Pen Wiper and Blotter
Embossed Leather Corners
18 x 24 in. $2.25 12 x 15 in. $2.00

No. 091. Writing Desk
36 in. wide, 18 in. deep, 46 in. high
Oak, $34.00 Mahogany, $42.00 Ash, $30.00

No. 027. Dining Chair
Heavy Leather Seat
18 in. wide, 17 in. deep, 37 in. high
Oak, $10.00 Mahogany, $12.00 Ash, $9.50

No. 01. Sideboard. 15-inch mirror
66 inches wide 28 inches deep 40 inches high
Oak, $80.00 Mahogany, $95.00 Ash, $75.00

No. 029. Dining Chair
Leather Seat
19 in. wide, 18 in. deep, 38 in. high
Oak, $11.00 Mahogany, $13.50 Ash, $10.00

No. 010. Serving Table
44 in. wide, 22 in. deep, 36 in. high to shelf
Oak, $15.00 Mahogany, $18.00 Ash, $14.00
With Drawer $3.50 extra

No. 089. Writing Desk
(Writing Pad on hinges)
40 in. wide, 24 in. deep
Oak, $28.00 Mahogany, $35.00 Ash, $25.00

No. 0106. Bedstead

Made in three-quarter and full sizes. Oak, $34.00 Mahogany, $42.00 Ash, $32.00

Box covered springs, $16.00 Mattress, $10.00

No. 085. Bookcase
66 in. wide, 62 in. high, 14 in. deep Oak, $70.00, Mahogany, $85.00, Ash, $66.00

No. 0101. Wood Box for fireplace. Hand-wrought iron or copper trimmings
48 inches wide 24 inches deep 24 inches high
Oak, $42.00 Mahogany, $50.00 Ash, $40.00

No. 039a. Low Rocker, Leather Seat
18 in. wide, 17 in. deep, 37 in. high

Oak	Mahogany	Ash
$10.00	$12.50	$9.50

No. 031. Hall Chair. Heavy leather seat
20 in. wide 19 in. deep 46 in. high
Oak, $18.00 Mahogany, $22.00 Ash, $16.00

No. 030. Bedroom Chair
Heavy leather padded seat
17 in. wide 17 in. deep 43 in. high
Oak, $11.00 Mahogany, $13.50 Ash, $10.00

No. 026. Dining Arm Chair
Heavy leather padded seat
24 in. wide, 20 in. deep, 18 in. to seat
26 in. back Oak, $16.00
Mahogany, $19.50 Ash, $15.00

No. 025. Dining Chair
Heavy leather padded seat 18 in. wide
17 in. deep 17 in. high to seat 20 in. back
Oak, $11.00 Mahogany, $13.50 Ash, $10.00

No. 0110. Dressing Table
39 in. wide, 18 in. deep, 30 in. high
Swinging Mirror 29 x 20 in.
Oak, $30.00 Mahogany, $37.00 Ash, $28.00

No. 040. Rocking Chair
Heavy Leather Seat
23 in. wide, 18 in. deep, 24 in. back
Oak, $16.00 Mahogany, $20.00 Ash, $15.00
Note.—This chair is also made with Leather Seat same as No. 039

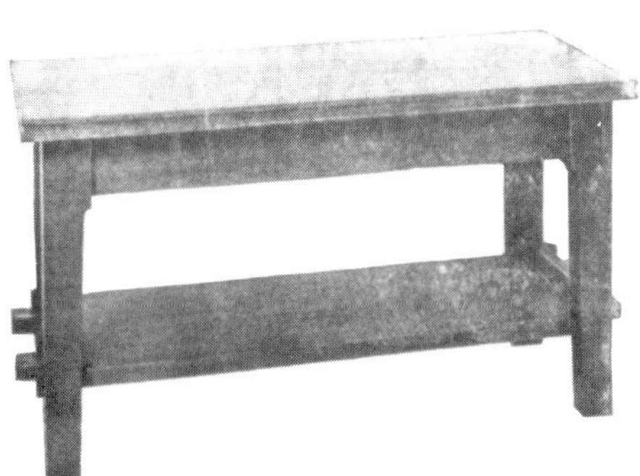

No. 071. Piano Bench
36 in. wide, 16 in. deep, 21 in. high
Oak, $12.00 Mahogany, $14.50 Ash, $10.00

No. 039. Rocking Chair
Leather Padded Seat
21 in. wide, 16 in. deep, 22 in. back
Oak, $16.00 Mahogany, $20.00 Ash, $15.00

No. 065½. Electric Chandelier. Five lights
Frame and chains hand-wrought copper. Opalescent glass shades. $36.00

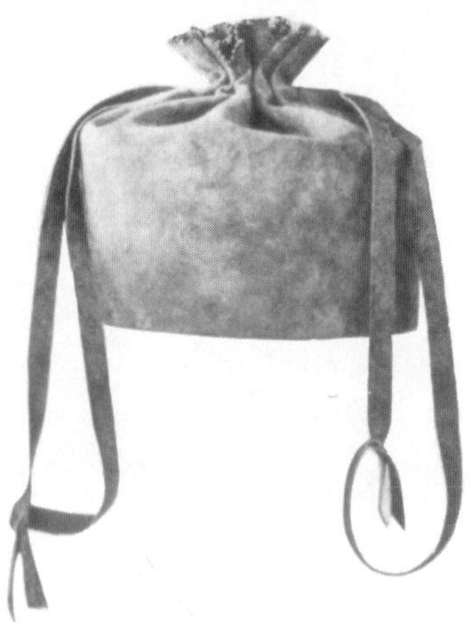

No. 0124. Leather Collar Bag, Ooze Calf
Green, Gray, Red and Brown Colors
$1.50

No. 073½. Round Table
30 inches Diameter, 29½ inches high
Oak, $25.00; Mahogany, $31.00; Ash, $24.00
36 inches Diameter, 30 inches High
Oak, $28.00; Mahogany, $34.00; Ash, $27.00

No. 067. Chandelier. Gas
Hand-wrought iron. Four lights
$40.00

INTERIOR OF BLACKSMITH SHOP

SHOWING SOME SAMPLES OF FURNITURE TRIMMINGS
IN HAND-WROUGHT COPPER AND IRON

No. 072. Library Table
50 in. wide, 32 in. deep, 30 in. high
Oak, $25.00 Mahogany, $30.00
Ash, $23.00

No. 012. Dining Table "solid"
48 in. and 54 in. diameter 30 inches high
Oak, $48.00 & $52.00 Mahogany, $58.00 & $62.00
Ash, $46.00 and $50.00

No. 013. Extension Dining Table
48 inches in diameter, open 8 feet
Oak, $56.00 Mahogany, $66.00 Ash, $53.00
54 inches in diameter, open 9 feet
Oak, $58.00 Mahogany, $68.00 Ash, $55.00

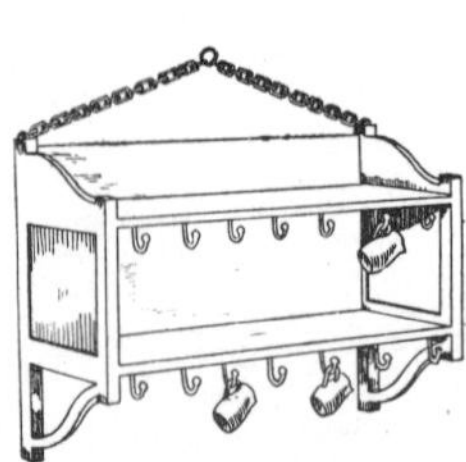

No. 020. Hanging Plate Rack
Hand-wrought Iron Chain and Cup Hangers
30 in. wide, 7 in. deep, 26 in. high
Oak, $19.00 Mahogany, $23.00
Ash, $18.00

No. 0109. Dresser
42 in. wide, 24 in. deep, 32 in. high
Hanging Mirror, 34 x 28 in.
Copper Candlesticks, Chain and Trimmings
Oak, $50.00 Mahogany, $62.00 Ash, $48.00

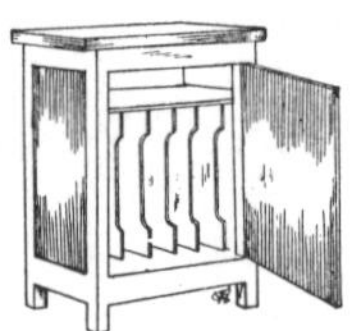

No. 0114. Music Cabinet
24 in. wide, 16 in. deep, 32 in. high
Oak, $22.00 Mahogany, $27.00 Ash, $20.00

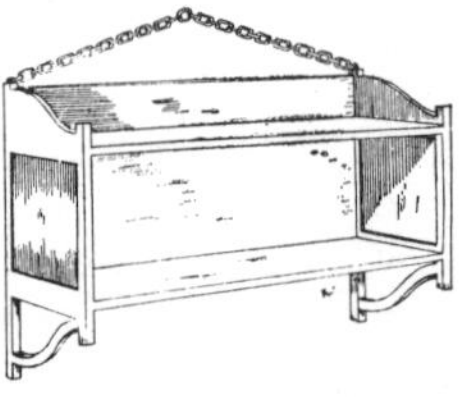

No. 021. Hanging Shelves
Hand-wrought Copper Chain
30 in. wide, 7 in. deep, 26 in. high
Oak, $17.00 Mahogany, $21.00 Ash, $16.00

No. 0100. Bride's Chest
Copper Trimmings
40 in. wide, 22 in. deep, 19 in. high
Oak, $32.00 Mahogany, $39.00 Ash, $30.00

No. 082. Bookcase
52 in. wide, 62 in. high, 13½ in. deep
Oak, $50.00 Mahogany, $60.00 Ash, $48.00

No. 087. Bookshelves
38 in. wide, 40 in. high, 12 in. deep
Oak, $24.00 Mahogany, $30.00 Ash, $22.00

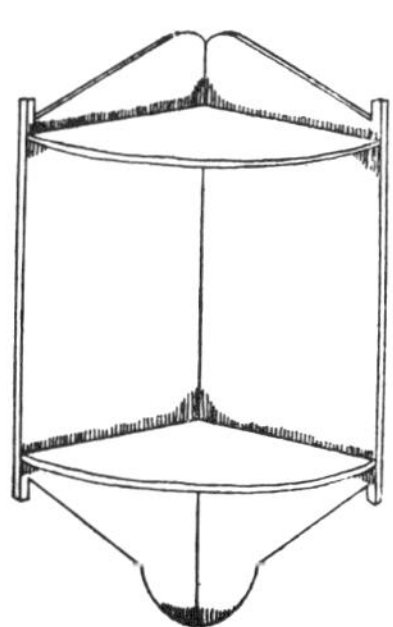

No. 024. Corner Shelf
Sides, 10 in. wide, 24 in. high
Oak, $6.50 Mahogany, $8.00 Ash, $6.00

No. 083. Bookcase
38 in. wide, 62 in. high, 13½ in. deep
Oak, $45.00 Mahogany, $55.00 Ash, $43.00

No. 015. Extension Dining Table
54 inches diameter to open 9 feet
Oak, $58.00 Mahogany, $68.00 Ash, $55.00

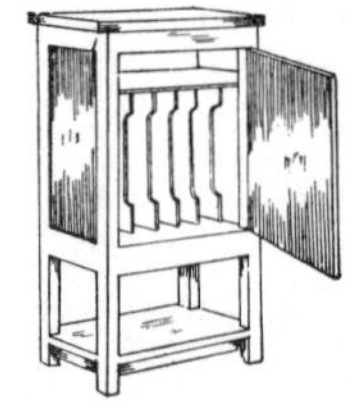

No. 0115. Music Cabinet
24 in. wide 16 in. deep 39 in. high
Oak, $25.00 Mahogany, $30.00
Ash, $23.00

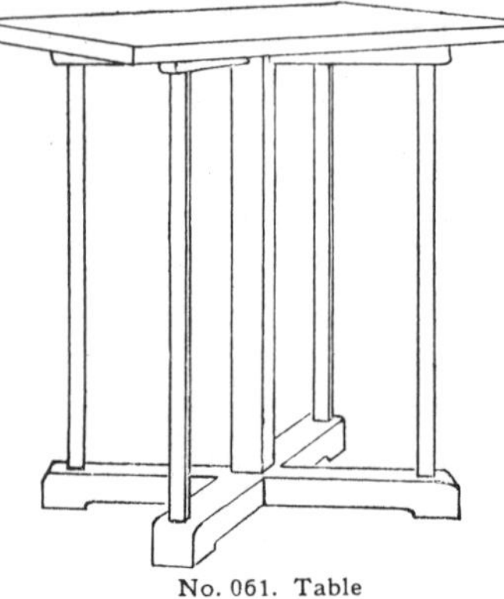

No. 061. Table
Top 20 x 30 inches 29 inches high
Oak, $20.00 Mahogany, $25.00 Ash, $18.00

No. 016. Extension Table
48 inches diameter to open 8 feet.
Oak, $50.00 Mahogany, $60.00 Ash, $48.00

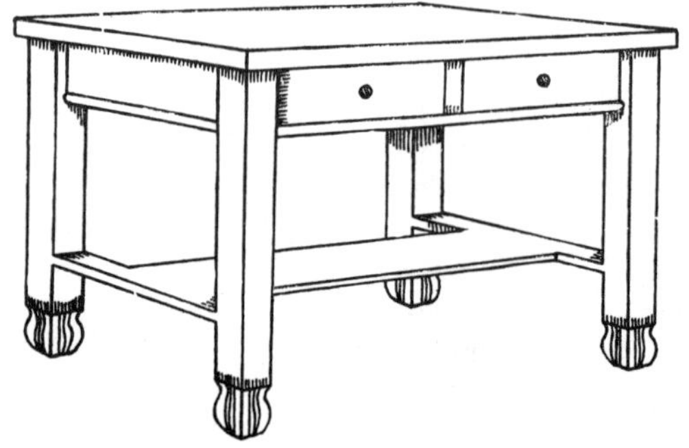

No. 076. Library Table
42 inches wide 30 inches deep 30 inches high
Oak, $35.00 Mahogany, $42.00 Ash, $33.00

No. 056. Office Desk
60 in. wide, 30 in. deep, 30 in. high
Oak, $65.00 Mahogany, $80.00 Ash, $60.00

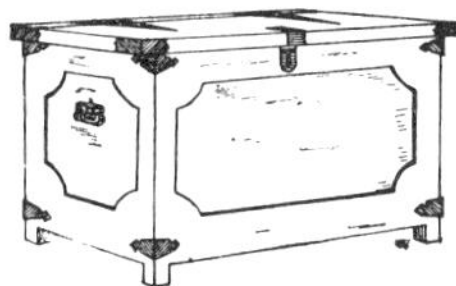

No. 099. Bride's Chest
40 in. wide, 22 in. deep, 19 in. high
Copper Trimmings
Oak, $30.00 Mahogany, $37.00 Ash, $28.00

No. 088. Hanging Bookshelves
36 in. wide, 38 in. high, 12 in. deep
Oak, $25.00 Mahogany, $30.00 Ash, 23.00

No. 062. Typewriter Desk
42 in. wide, 31 in. deep, 30½ in. high, 25 in. high to shelf
Oak, $38.00 Mahogany, $45.00 Ash, $36.00

No. 081. Bookcase
52 in. wide, 13 in. deep, 62 in. high
Oak, $50.00 Mahogany, $60.00, Ash, $48.00

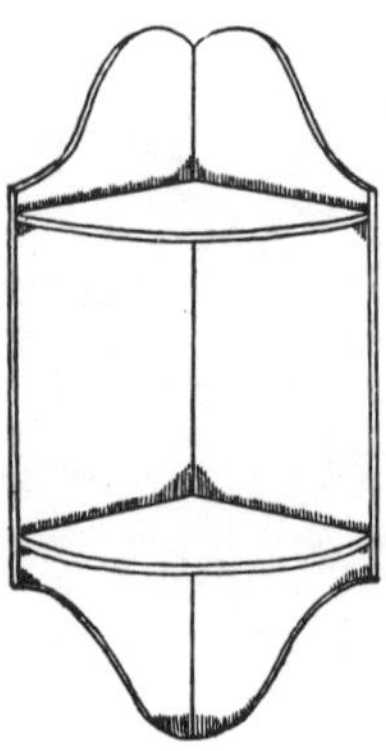

No. 023. Corner Shelf
Sides, 10 in. wide, 27 in. high
Oak, $6.00 Mahogany, $7.50 Ash, $5.50

No. 064. Wrought-iron Umbrella Stand
10 in. square, 28 in. high
$10.00

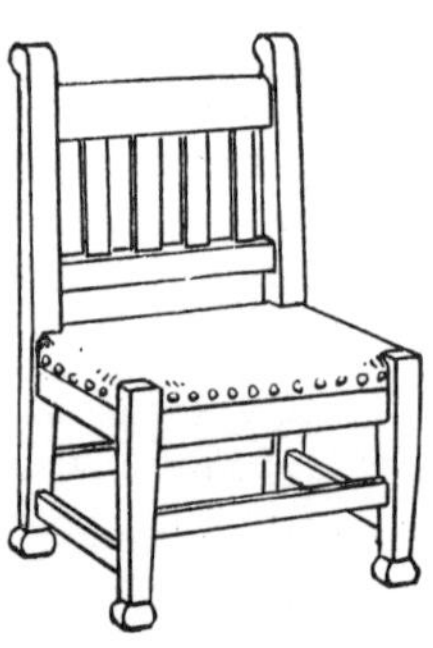

No. 037. Slipper Chair
14 in. wide, 13 in. deep, 13 in. to seat, 16-in. back
Oak, $9.00 Mahogany, $11.00 Ash, $8.50

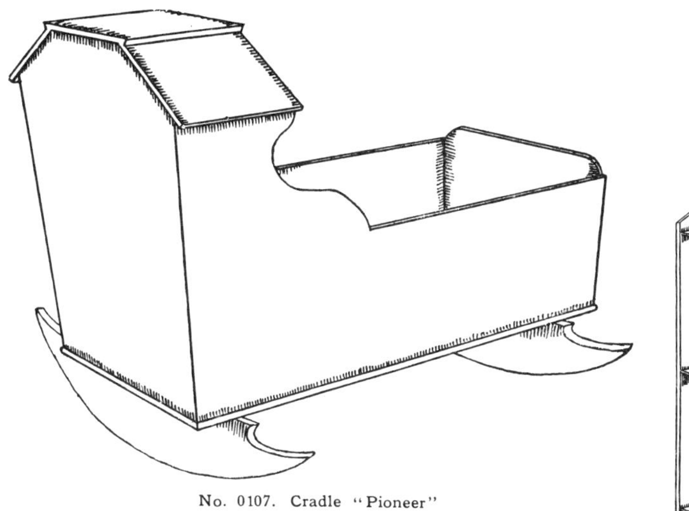

No. 0107. Cradle "Pioneer"

Oak, $18.00 Mahogany, $22.00 Ash, $16.00

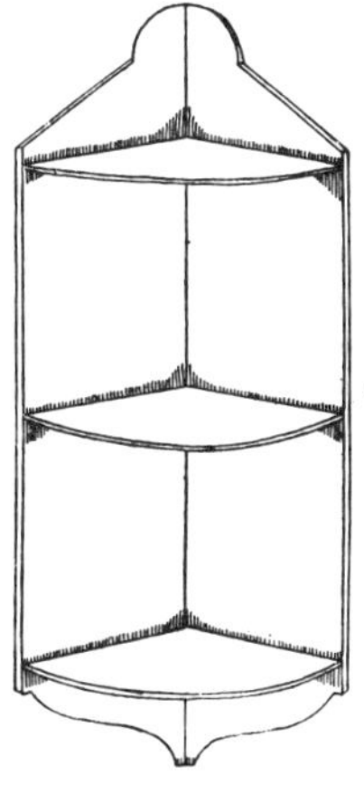

No. 022. Corner Shelf

Sides, 10 in. wide, 36 in. high

Oak, $7.00 Mahogany, $8.50

Ash, $6.50

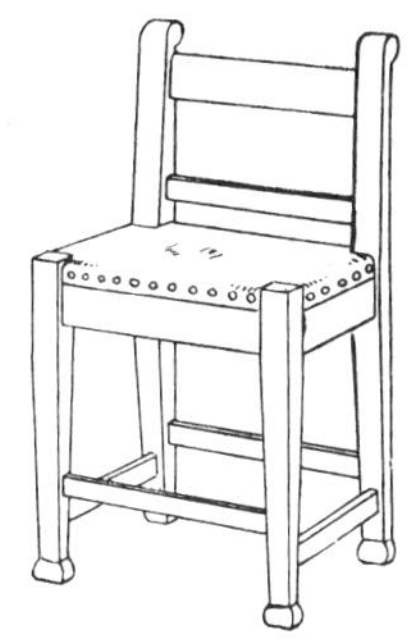

No. 035. Marshall P. Wilder Chair

For Dressing Table

Oak, $10.00 Mahogany, $12.00

Ash, $9.50

No. 0104. Bedstead

Made in two sizes—three-quarters and full size

Oak, $30.00 Mahogany, $37.00 Ash, $28.00

Box-covered Springs, $16.00

Mattress, $10.00

No. 057. Double Flat Desk

60 in. wide, 54 in. deep, 30 in. high

Oak, $100.00 Mahogany, $125.00 Ash, $90.00

No. 092. Writing Desk

40 in. wide, 15 in. deep, 54 in. high

Oak, $40.00 Mahogany, $50.00 Ash, $37.00

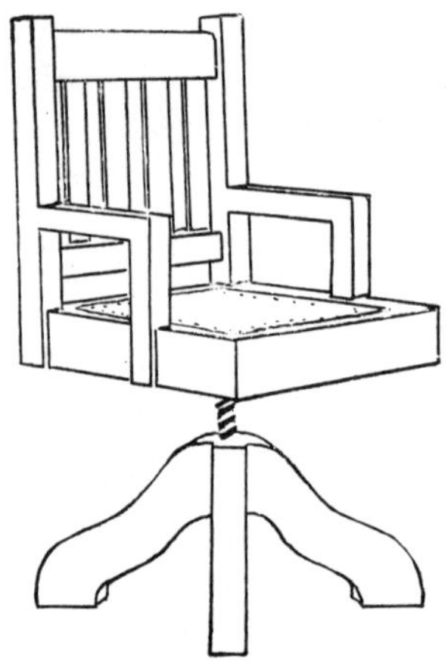

No. 038. Desk Chair

Leather Seat

22 in. wide, 18 in. deep, 20 in. back

Oak, $22.00 Mahogany, $27.00 Ash, $20.00

No. 04. Sideboard
66 in. wide, 28 in. deep, 38 in. high to shelf
18-in. Mirror
Oak, $90.00 Mahogany, $112.00 Ash, $84.00

No. 0112. Chiffonier
40 in. wide, 20 in. deep, 50 in. high
Oak, $42.00 Mahogany, $52.00 Ash, $40.00

No. 0103. Double Deck Bedstead
Box Covered Springs, $14.00 each
Mattress, $10.00 each
84 in. long, 42 in. wide, 80 in. high
Oak, $40.00, Mahogany, $48.00, Ash, $37.00

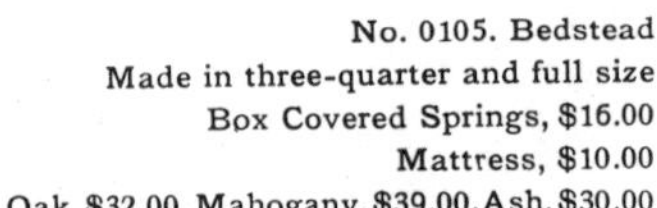

No. 0105. Bedstead
Made in three-quarter and full size
Box Covered Springs, $16.00
Mattress, $10.00
Oak, $32.00, Mahogany, $39.00, Ash, $30.00

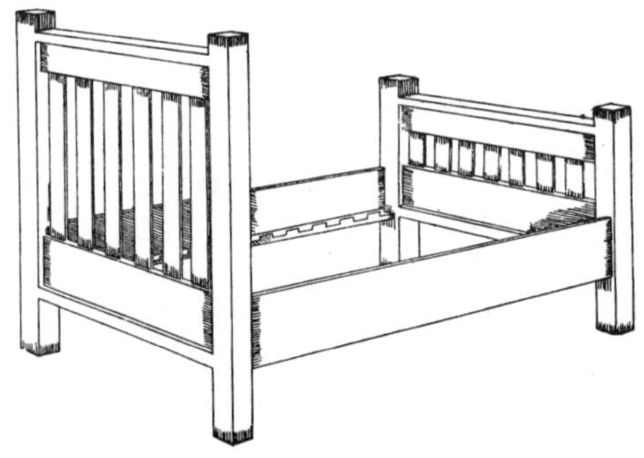

No. 07. China Cabinet
Clear glass set in copper. Copper trimmings
40 inches wide 18 inches deep 64 inches high
Oak, $75.00 Mahogany, $90.00 Ash, $70.00

No. 0102. Gun Cabinet
36 inches wide 14 inches deep 66 inches high
Oak, $75.00 Mahogany, $90.00 Ash, $70.00

No. 095. Settee, Spring Seat, Leather Cushions
76 in. wide, 26 in. deep, 38 in. high
Oak, $85.00 Mahogany, $95.00 Ash, $82.00
Pillows extra Other sizes made to order

No. 094. Settee, Spring Seat, Leather Cushions
76 in. wide, 26 in. deep, 38 in. high
Oak, $85.00 Mahogany, $95.00 Ash, $82.00
Pillows extra Other sizes made to order

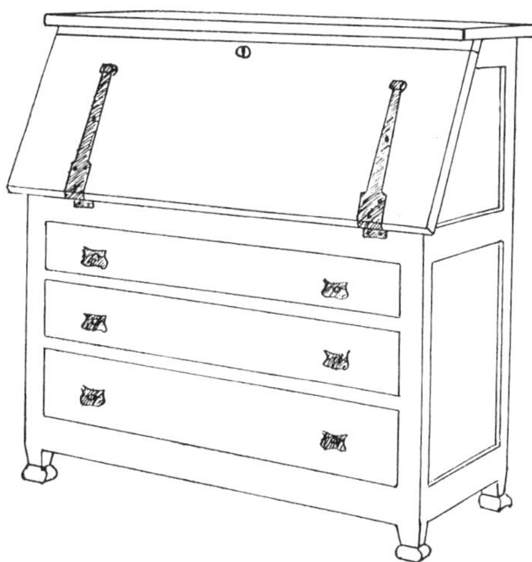

No. 058. Writing Desk
42 in. wide, 20 in. deep, 49 in. high
Oak, $50.00 Mahogany, $60.00 Ash, $48.00

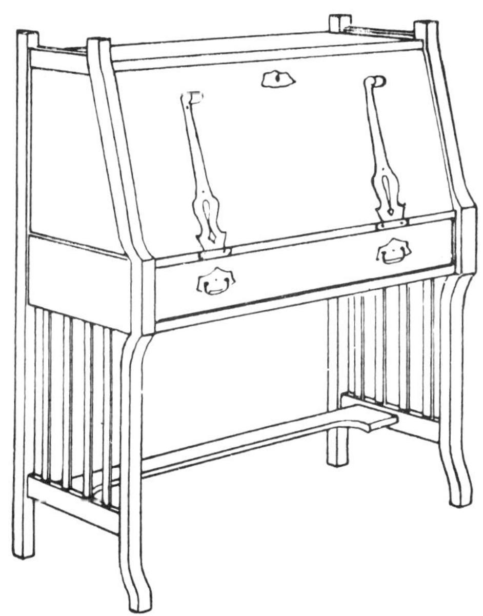

No. 059. Writing Desk
36 in. wide, 16 in. deep, 46 in. high
Oak, $40.00 Mahogany, $48.00 Ash, $38.00

No. 060. Hall Seat and Mirror
50 inches wide 20 inches deep 62 inches high to center of glass
Oak, $54.00 Mahogany, $65.00 Ash, $50.00

Roycroft Straddle Chair

Did You Ever See One? No!
Well, You Have Missed It.

Induces Sound Sleep, an Easy Conscience and a Good Appetite

Oak, $12.50 Mahogany, $15.50 Ash, $11.50